Climbing to Go Nowhere

Autobiography

Wanda Jernigan

outskirts press

I would like to take the time to thank the following
individuals for supporting me in writing my book

I would like to give special thanks to my Mom and Dad
for making me the strong person that I am today.

I would like to also thank my three children DJ, PJ, and Charlotte for
giving me the opportunity to show them that anything is possible.

I would like to thank my Best Friend and Soulmate David
Hughes for pushing me towards completing this book

I would also like to thank my special friends and colleagues Brenda
Sutton, Joyce Clements, Iristine Cross, and Linda Rushing.

My friend Wanda Baker whom I just lost this
year and my Best Friend Darlene Bagley.

ONCE UPON ANOTHER decade in the year 1959 a child was born to Abraham and Ethel Jones. They were in love–as they thought--at the time of the birth of their 1st child. Ethel was the type of woman who thought all things were to be the way her husband wanted them. The two had small disagreements about what to name the new child. Ethel's idea of a name was to name her after both her grandparents and Abraham's idea of a name was to be Wanda, if a girl, because he wandered through life. Never heard them mention any boys' name. So, Wanda was her name.

After the age of eight, I remember my father making me work with him on weekends and every day that I was not in school. He worked from 6:00 am until whenever. He farmed and was a contractor by trade. So, I had to help him with whatever he needed. It ranged from driving farm equipment to using a wheelbarrow or shovel. It did not matter, you just did it. He worked me just like a man all those years. It was tough as a little girl and later as a teenager.

As the years passed by and I became a teenager, I learned many things about my parents by watching how they acted together. My father was a man who was very demanding, and my mother just went along with it, never taking up for herself. My father was always about work and very little play. After raising a few of her siblings before marrying my dad, Mom thought this would somehow relieve her of raising kids. Much to her surprise it did not fall that way. Now she had the responsibility of taking care of a newborn that was hers. Oh Boy!! Her life became a challenge in many ways. At that time, it was not so much about depression even though I knew she had it. I listened to her many stories over the years as I was growing up with my other two sisters who came along later–Joyce being the middle one and Patty the baby. Yes, I eventually realized that Mom never wanted any kids at all. I was not sure at first how to handle this fact. After I learned more about my mom's life, I understood why she felt this way. She was from a family that did not talk about sex, boys, and such issues. Not even knowing how to avoid pregnancy, led to many of the problems that she experienced. So, having to grow up and not live the life of a teenager had to be tough for her or anyone placed in that situation.

I always thought things between my parents were generally good. However, as I was getting close to 11 years of age, I can remember my father calling my mom names and telling her how stupid she was. By then I knew what those words meant and could not really believe he would talk to her that way. Mom never said a word back to him. Now I know it was the fear she carried. As a child at my age, I knew what he said to her was wrong. My mom was not stupid and was a good worker and always put 100 percent into anything she did. This is when I started to see another side of my Father I had never seen. I remember telling him, "Do not talk to my mom that way."

He looked at me as though he could have put his foot right up my behind. But I never heard him call her that again where I could hear it.

Later, after talking to my mom I found out he did a lot more things to her that NO woman should have to go through.

As my body began to change in many ways, I did not realize what was happening because I had no guidance. I can remember the day I started my period. I was at school with a pair of white shorts on and did not even know what was happening. I remember getting on the bus and the driver telling me to wrap my sweater around my mid-section. She then asked me to sit behind her so she could talk to me. That is how I found out about the female monthly cycle. It should not have been that way. Again, this was my life. By the time I got home I was so angry with my mom for never even talking to us about this. How can a mother not let her children know what a girl faces as a teenager and the risk and causes of things like pregnancy and STDs? If she had talked to us about her situations in life that would have helped us in the long run. It may have not changed what happened in our lives but maybe we would have taken different directions. I had to learn that she could not tell us because she never had the guidance in her life. I realized then that both Mom and us kids had been deprived of a lot in our lives as girls and as women.

Around 1973-1974 my parents decided to end the marriage after 15 years. It was the hardest thing on my sisters and me. I will never forget having to read that letter my mother left on the table with the supper she prepared before she walked out. My father only attended school to the 5th grade, so I had to read the letter in front of him and my siblings.

The words hit me so hard because that is when I realized that my mom never really wanted any children at all. However, she did her job as a mom for us.

My two sisters went to live with my mom, and I stayed with my dad. From this day forward I cleaned and cooked for my dad. I went to school and worked a job on the outside. My Dad did his best to try to keep me so busy that I would not have time to have a life. It worked well for a year. And it was a year or more before I ever saw my mom. No contact or even a call to check on me. It hurt, but I could not let that control my life. When I say I catered to a man, I did for my dad as if I was married to him. Later, you will see why that was a mistake in my life.

Let me begin with the year 1975 when I met a friend named Terri. We were always together and did a lot of things as one. Terri was dating this guy named Alan and he had a friend named TP. They decided it was a good idea to hook me up with him for a date. So, they picked me up from my house in a small town called Zuni, Virginia. I was 16 going on 17, I believe. We all went riding around, hanging out and talking. TP and I were trying to get to know each other. The age difference between the two of us was probably three to four years. Yes, I was nervous to be with him. For one he was older and more experienced with things. Me, shy and knowing nothing about relationships. My father was totally against me being with him. The only way I got to go was if Terri was there. I guess he trusted my friend would make sure I was safe. I continued to see TP for a few months. TP was a man with whom I should have taken a chance. If only I had known more about relationships and womanhood, I probably would have taken a chance with him. TP was a fantastic gentleman and a wonderful person. He never tried to push me into anything even though he was older. I had the utmost respect for him as a man. Sorry, TP. Best wishes in your life and good luck!

My sister, Joyce, was coming to spend a night with me for the first time in a while. I still could not understand why my sister Patty was not allowed to come. I guess my mom figured she was too young to be with us. Never really knew why. My Dad knew I had a date with this guy John from Smithfield. He told me he needed me to go to Suffolk and pick Joyce up from the Suffolk Moose lodge. So, I called John to make sure we could do that, and he said it was no problem. John seemed to be a cool person and was very nice so off we went.

When we arrived around eight that night I had to go inside. I went in and told the person at the door why I was there. They paged her name over the intercom to come to the front. I waited 15 minutes and no Joyce. So, I asked them to page her again. This time some young man came up to me to ask me why I was looking for her. I told him she was my sister, and I was there to pick her up. So, he offered to help me find her. The whole time I believe he knew where she was. He was just buying time with me. I excused myself and went outside to let John know she was not answering. I told him I would go back and try one more time before I called my dad, which was something I did not want to do. Once again, this guy met me at the door as I came back in. He asked me if I was there by myself, and I stated no. So finally, here came my sister like she had been in there the whole time. NOT!!! So, she wanted to stay and have some guy bring her home. I did not want to agree to it because my dad might find out. But I gave in and said OK. So, twenty minutes to thirty minutes passed and I said, "I must go; someone is waiting for me outside."

Peter, the guy I'd met while waiting for my sister offered to walk me to the car.

I said, "That's ok, I am with someone.

Peter said, "So what? I will knock him out; then you can go with me."

I walked away and told him, "Just stay where you are."

He didn't want to, but I said please. I guess it worked that time.

When I came outside to get in the car with John he was upset. He started asking me a lot of questions like why I stayed in there so long. I tried to explain the whole thing to him. At this point he was mad, so there was no use explaining anything. Of course, I had a time to be home so the two of us really did not have a lot of time left before I had to be home. So, we were going down 460 to Zuni and he had his car going about 80 to 100 miles per hour. I told him if he did not slow down, he could pull over and let me out. I did not want to die that way. I had to keep telling him how sorry I was for him to calm down. Finally, after a reckless 15-minute ride, all I wanted was to just be home and my sister to be there when I got there.

Well, to my surprise she was not. I had to pretend to be asleep with her in the bed as well. She showed up at one or two in the morning tapping on my bedroom window. I let her in and said, "Goodnight, we will talk in the morning."

Then things changed. I went to stay with my mom after a year of not seeing her or talking to her since the divorce. I was excited I was going. My sisters were still living with her. Upon their divorce I felt I should stay with my dad because years prior to this my father had open heart surgery. It was then I felt he needed me more than did my mom. Later, down the road you will see how this hurt me in a lot of ways and in relationships.

When I arrived at my mom's, I was excited to see her. Then I had to meet my stepfather. I never saw eye to eye with him. But just seeing my sisters and Mom was a wonderful feeling. As I got settled in and was able to talk to my sister, I realized she knew this guy, Peter, I had spoken to at the Suffolk Moose Lodge. We talked for hours about him. However, I wish she had told me everything. I guess she figured I liked him so why ruin it for me? I met him later that weekend when he came over to my mom's, (without her permission of course). Boy, was that something when she found out. Anyway, we laughed about things the whole weekend until it was time for me to go.

Peter got my phone number from my sister and called me, and we continued to talk for a few weeks. Peter asked me if it was OK to come by my house and of course I asked my dad. He was good with it if he knew when he was coming. Father was very protective of me and wanted only the best for me. At that time, I just felt he was smothering me and not letting me have a life.

We continued to see each other for many months and things started to get heated between the two of us. Since I was still a virgin, I was scared to death of the whole situation with him. I was able to maintain for six months before I gave in. I felt this man cared and loved me enough that he would be there with me to the end of time. If someone tells you it is a beautiful moment, it is not. Or maybe it was because of the person that it involved. Who knows? Being so young I still knew very little about sex. It just seemed so unfair not having someone in your life to teach you about the birds and bees. I pictured the whole experience as a passionate and caring situation. I knew there might be some pain as well as a very happy moment. At least that is what I pictured just from reading books about it. How wrong was I? I began to learn a lot of things from that day forward that I did not even want to know or experience. Peter and I continued to see each other until the unexpected happened....

I remember Peter calling me and asking me to come to where he was living at the time, and I agreed to sneak out of my house and tell my father I was going to a girlfriend's house. That was never the case. I met Peter at his house to find out no one was there but the two of us. I believe he planned it that way, but I would never know for sure. All was good and then one thing led to another, and all my dreams of a faithful marriage ended that day. I always dreamed that when I got that chance to make love to someone I cared about and wanted to marry it would be so romantic. The passion I dreamed of was not even close to what I thought it would be.

I felt as though my world was out of control. Up until this year I'd had big dreams of going to college with my classmates, but I decided to drop out of school because of Peter. Then I felt so guilty of dropping out that I got my life together and went back to school the last four months of my senior year and buckled down hard. It was a rough time but when all was said and done, I graduated June 1977 with my class and my dad was so proud of what I had done. Little to my surprise, he would never get to see my two sisters graduate.

On August 4, 1977, my father passed at the age of 37. It was more than I thought I could bear at the time and could not understand why. It hurt me so bad to know that I had just seen him hours before. It should have been my time to be able to enjoy adult time doing things with my father, not preparing a funeral. When he died a part of me went with him. However, I had to learn to stand on my own two feet now. I had to grow up so fast and learn a lot of things on my own as I went.

The mistakes I made from here on out destroyed my soul in a lot of ways. Yes, I was now with my man or at least I thought so, until I found out all he was about was moving from woman to woman. He did not know how to be faithful to one. I guess he saw me as a weak woman looking for love. After the loss of my father, I found out one month later I was pregnant. If only my dad had known, things may have been different. I was so shocked and hurt for putting myself in that situation. However, I had no family guidance in my life to tell me what to do and not do. So now my whole life had changed, and I was in an awful situation. What should I do? I was confused and mad at myself for giving in to Peter.

I had no other choice but to tell Peter. I was 18 now and homeless at the same time. I had no other choice but to move in with him. Things were good at first; then he started hanging out late and saying he was with the guys. What was I to believe? Months went by and soon it would be time for me to have the baby.

That was when I found out my boyfriend had been arrested for stealing and sexual battery. It almost sent me over the edge. He was a man I thought I knew. While he was in jail, they dropped the stealing charge because the sexual charge carried more prison time. He was charged with that because they railroaded him. He was only guilty of stealing. The woman he was involved with got her daughter to lie because she found out about me.

So, for the next months until Brandon was born Peter was locked up. They made only one exception, allowing him to come to the hospital to see the baby when he arrived in this world. Brandon was such a joy and a beautiful child. I was happy and confused at the time. Here I was getting ready to be MOM and knew nothing of how to be one. It was something I would have to grow to understand.

Well, after the baby was born, I moved out of the Jones's house to my aunt's house where she helped me with Brandon while I worked. I worked 3rd shift and she would watch him for me until 2:00 or 3:00 in the afternoon. Peter and I stopped seeing each other and I became depressed because I had a child now and no father in his life. I became so upset with it that I tried to keep up with Peter and failed to realize I should have put time into Brandon instead of his no-good father. Things seemed so unfair to me. However, my uncle said I had to straighten up or move out. So back to Mrs. Jones house I went.

I stayed with Peter and began trying to change him. Nothing I did or said worked. I had to accept that he was what he was: an unfaithful man. And I would soon learn that it just was not in his mind or lifestyle to be a good man. I guess I was so blind that I could not see that I deserved better. But I was also so afraid to be on my own and alone again. Self-esteem is something that can be destroyed if you lose faith in yourself. I did and I wish I'd gotten support from counseling then when I was going through all this drama. I felt like I just needed a huge balloon, and this would carry me away from all the heartache. However, it did not work.

I started to think about things, and I felt it wasn't fair for my son to live without a father in his life and I was still young and hurt and confused about everything. I went to the Social Service office to see if I could get help. They seemed to offer very little, and it was like what do I do? I talked to them for many hours. I then decided to put him up for adoption. I tried this twice before I finally did it. My whole life changed for the worse after that. I tried not to look back over what I had done but I could not erase it from my mind. What had I done and why? Because of a man.

A few years later Peter and I hooked back up again. I never knew why I took him back. I always thought it was because I loved him. I imagined maybe there was a chance that he had thought about things, and we could try to get Brandon back. But he claimed that the child would be better with the family he was with. It hurt but I had Peter back--at least, I thought, for now.

Peter asked me to marry him, and I really thought things would be so much better. Things were good for about a year, until I found out he ran around on me. Then I learned he did this the second day after we were married. How could I be so dam stupid to continue to deal with this man? I guess I just enjoyed being used. Why?

Of course, being the man, he denied it all. Months went by again and he kept telling me he wanted me to have another baby. I could not believe he would ask that of me. I was still hurting and thinking about my other son. I just did not want to. So, I kept sneaking my birth control pills and hiding them. He was getting upset because I was not becoming pregnant. One day I was gone, and he went into my clothes drawer for something. I never knew for what. Well, he found my pills and became very angry that I had lied to him. So, for the next 30 days or more he made sure we had sex whether I wanted it or not. His words to me were, "You will get pregnant because I won't stop until you do. It was the most miserable time for me until it finally happened.

Then once I found out for sure I was pregnant, the nightmares started all over for me again. He started hanging out drinking and running with women. Peter and I lived in an apartment in Suffolk. I was working at a dealership so I could make sure I provided for myself and to be able to get things that I was going to need for the baby. There were so many nights that I cried myself to sleep because of him. I figured since I was working at the dealership and learning new things it would help with the void in my life.

Peter would pick me up some days instead of letting me drive. I could not understand why. Well, we continued to see each other, and the only bright spot was learning my job potential. I was smarter than I thought, though I hid it well!! My boss decided he wanted me to train in the parts department since it was an opening coming up and he knew I was a fast learner. And of course, it would be more money per hour. I was excited about this opportunity. SO, for the next few months I continued to learn my new job and was able to support the service department in helping the mechanics out. I became close to all the fellows, and they appreciated me helping them and we all worked well together.

I became close to two of the guys that worked there so I was able to talk to them about everything. I will never forget one of them telling me I was such a hard worker and honest person that my husband did not deserve me. Bill was an older gentleman and married so I listened to him. I knew he had to know what he was talking about. He was a man who was about family and devotion so I could trust him. He told me I should move on with my life because I deserved better. For the next few months all I could do was think about what he said. I was not for sure if the other guy that was always with Bill was talking about me. So, I was afraid to take that leap of Faith.

Then it happened again–another woman with my husband. This time I just could not deal with it anymore. Especially being married, I thought you were supposed to be faithful to your spouse. I guess loyalty was just not in his vocabulary. So, we continued to stay together but my feelings were changing toward him each day. I guess all I could think about was my son being without a father.

Well, while I was working, the other guy that I used to talk to started to notice a change in me. He said, "Wanda, you just need to let all that negative stuff in your life go and move on."

To my surprise this guy was about to let all of us know he'd decided to go back home in Colorado. Yes, he was cute and single, but I was married and in love. Well, the department decided to have a going away party for him, so I got with the ladies in the department to see what they wanted to do. We all decided to buy him a sweater since we knew it was cold there. So, I volunteered to do the shopping, and everyone could pitch in with the cost. Well, he was leaving before pay day, so I knew my mother-in-law had an account with JC Penney. So, I asked her if I could charge it on her account and pay for it on Friday. And I explained to her what WE all were doing. She agreed.

The next thing I knew I was being accused of sleeping with the man and having sex with him? I was so hurt that my husband would accuse me of that. It was only to cover up what he was doing wrong. However, I learned later that his sister made a big issue about it to him. They never once asked anything about the facts--they just assumed. All I was doing was being the caring person I am. I had to agree he was cute, but I was married, and I took my vows seriously. More than I can say about my husband.

Well, it was the day of the party for Dale. So, Bill asked me if I was going to stay that day and I told him I would. Bill already knew that sometimes Peter would hit me or verbally abuse me, and he did not like it at all. So as the day progressed, and it was getting near the end of the day, the ladies asked me to help them set up and I did. In the process of getting things taken care of, some of the guys in the shop starting drinking and hanging around and talking. While I was helping, someone pulled me a drink, so I started sipping on mine and bringing out the food and all. Bill came to me and said, "Don't look now but your husband is trying to get your attention." Bill added, "All you need to do is tell us and we can have him removed from the property. I said, "No need for that. I will go outside and let him know I'll be ready in about an hour."

However, that was not in his plans for me. He wanted me to leave right then, and he said, "Do not force me to make a scene."

At first, I started to just let Bill come out and knock him out. But because I didn't like people in my business I decided to just go inside and tell them I had to go and to tell Dale goodbye. I felt it was the right thing to do since I was married. Well, to my surprise Dale used to stop by the bar that Peter's sister worked at, and he told her we all were going to come down later to drink. So, I guess he assumed something, though I did not know what at the time. If I had known for one second what was going to happen, I would have stayed.

Well, I left and all the way home he kept repeating, "You just wait until we get home."

I was scared because I knew what he could do to me. Once we got home and he opened the door to the apartment all hell broke loose. I had on a cute little sundress with flat shoes. The next thing I knew he grabbed my dress and ripped it off me. I was standing there with nothing but my slip, bra, and panties on. Then he grabbed me and told me to take the rest of it off. I could not believe what was happening. It was like a nightmare, but it was real. He forced himself on me and continued to bruise my neck. I had a line of hickies around my neck. When he finished, he said, "Now you can go and meet them and see what your friends will think now. I felt so dirty and cheap, I could barely stand. I felt like what he had done was so wrong, but what had I done to deserve that? So, I got dressed because he would not let me shower before I left, and I went back to the dealership as if nothing had happened. I felt so embarrassed, but I kept a straight face and wore a turtleneck so no one could see my neck. I left with the ladies, and we met everyone at the bar. I decided to sit at the bar since Peter's sister was working and watching me as well. Dale came over to talk to me to see if I was ok. I said yes and he sat beside me at the bar. He said, "You seem to be a little nervous with me sitting here."

I stated to him I was, and he asked me why. They all knew I was married so it was not like he was trying to jump my bones. Dale continued to question my nervousness til finally I broke down and told and let him know also that was his sister behind the bar. "Really!!" he said. He continued to tell me I needed to get out of that marriage because it was toxic. He was right but I could not see it until weeks later.

I had to finally realize that Peter was not going to change for me or anyone. So, I decided to move in with a lady that I had met. Nancy was single and had been through a breakup so I figured we would be good for each other. The two of us got an apartment downtown and we lived there with my son PJ.

Nancy and I lived together for almost a year. It was getting close to the time for me to be eligible for the inheritance that my father had left me, so I decided to try to buy me a trailer. I found a single wide trailer in Carrsville and purchased it. I decided to let Nancy move in with me since Peter and I were still separated. So, for the next year Nancy lived with PJ Jr. and me. Things went well and Nancy and I would hang out a lot with some friends. I thought it was all good for a while until I found out the guy, she was talking to was married and his wife's name was Nancy as well. How convenient you might say. She wanted me to talk or have something to do with the friend, but I knew he was married. This was something I was totally against because of my marriage to Peter. I would go with her from time to time to the Shady Grove and have a few beers with the gang. However, that was it.

Nancy became obsessed with this guy to the point he had her doing drugs and partying all the time. It was too much for me to deal with, so I had to ask her to move out. She did and it was years later before I saw her again. I could not believe it was her. Drugs sure take you down a hard road. To my surprise I would find out more about drugs later in my life.

Then one day after she had moved out Peter showed up. He wanted to see if there was a chance, we could give our marriage another try. Well, I just hung in there for about one more year until his brother showed up at our house. His brother, John, came by to see Peter only to find out he was not home, though Peter had asked him to come by. John went to the store and got two 8-packs of Pony Millers. He waited for his brother for about two hours and left. He left me one of the 8 pack of beers. That was the night that I drank all eight of them and fell in the front yard and asked God to help me get out of that lifestyle. I got sick and went to bed.

Peter came home that night around one or later. He had not been home any more than an hour and we got a call from his sister that his brother, John, had been shot. So off to Norfolk General we went.

I had made up my mind that morning on the way back home that it was over for me. I could not do it anymore. However, as a wife I could not leave him then because of what had happened to his brother. So, I stayed in it until his brother passed and everything had settled down for about a month.

He stayed out one night during that month, and I woke up early the next morning, packed his clothes and put them at the back door. When he came in that morning around nine, I asked him to take his clothes and to get out. I heard the same old song and dance: "I will change; it won't happen again." After more than fifty times of trying I just did not have it in me anymore. I was done.

Even though I did not realize certain things about myself, others around me noticed how things were taking a toll on me. PJ's father was never in his life. I raised him by myself without a bit of child support. Or should I say the only time I got any money was when he was arrested and made to pay a certain amount. After that the amount slowly declined more and more.

He continued to try and get me to go back with him, but I stood my ground and moved on. We were still married but not living with each other. He continued to harass me on my job.

By now I felt I had been away from Peter long enough to be safe. I got a new job working at a different dealership working in parts. My new boss, Earl, was a fantastic boss. He taught me a lot of things and talked to me about a lot of things in general. As a man, my boss taught me more in my year working with him than my own Father did. He helped me to get my life back on track and learn to be happy with myself. Thanks, Earl, you will never be forgotten. Day in and day out I waited on the mechanics so they could fix customers' cars to make a living for them or their families. So, for the next few months my boss kept telling me this one mechanic was eyeing me.

I said, "No, I don't think so."

Yeah, he was cute, but I did not feel like I'd been out of my situation long enough, plus I was still legally married to Peter though separated. Then it started all over again Peter kept calling and coming to the dealership trying to get me to go back with him. I almost did but then I thought about all the horrible things that had happened and I said no. Finally, my boss told him if he did not stop, he would arrange it so he could never step on the property again. So then is when he realized it was over.

He passed on September 4, 2004.

Earl kept talking to me about trying to get my life back on track and going out again. I wanted to but I was afraid I was not healed enough yet. Anyway, finally this guy got up enough nerve to start talking to me. He invited me to go to lunch and we would go to this lake and eat lunch and then go back to work. He seemed nice enough, so we continued to talk, and I found out he played music in a band. I really thought that was so cool. Well, we continued to talk, and he had a show coming up in two weeks and asked me if I would like to come.

I said, "I don't have the money for that."

He said, "Don't worry about that; I can get you in and if you want anything to drink, I will have them put it on my tab. So, I got my sister Joyce to drive me over there that night in Newport News to watch him play and sing music. It was nice and relaxing, and it had been months since I'd been out. Well, the night was coming to an end and CA asked me to ride home with him. I was not sure at first but since I knew him from work, I felt I would be safe. My son was spending the night with a friend, so I did not have to worry about going straight home. He asked me what I wanted to do, and I said, "I don't know; it's late and pretty much everything is closed."

All I could think about was getting even with my husband who was now my ex for all he had done to me. So, my next move was not a smart one only a get even tactic. We ended up at a hotel that night and I was not sure that is what I wanted yet. Well, the longer we spent talking to each other, the more I felt that maybe it was time to be involved with him. We had spent a lot of time together at work and away from work. What did I have to lose?

He drove me home the next morning so I could go and pick up my son. He kissed me goodbye and said he really had a great evening, and he would see me later. And he did. We spent that afternoon together with my son and me. We continued to spend time together and I would go to his events and hang out with the other ladies whose boyfriend or husband played with CA. All seemed well and we continued to see each other for about 11 months.

One Friday I remembered he told me he would not see me that weekend because he was playing out of town, I do believe. However, it got back to me he was messing with some girl. I was not there so I did not know for sure. However, I knew the person that told me had no reason to lie. So, I had some friends of mine come by and pick me up and we all headed to Nags Head for the weekend. It started off with everyone partying and having a good time; then individuals started to pair off. Yeah, me right along with the group. Everyone went their way, and I guess we all had the same thing in mind. Again, I guess that was my way of getting even. However, it did not make me feel any better. Oh well, let's just bury the secret, right?

CA had to play at this lodge, and I went with him there. For some reason I had this crazy feeling come over me. I was standing at the door watching individuals come in and this one girl kept watching me. It was odd but I figured maybe she knew me. Anyway, she started a conversation and she wanted to know how I knew CA. I told her we were dating and the look on her face could have killed. So, I figured she must know him better than I thought. Anyway, the two of us got into a disagreement that night and I had been drinking so I left. Probably should not have been driving but then the adrenaline kicked in and I no longer felt high from the alcohol. His drummer must have seen my disagreement and he told me he needed a ride home to his parent's house. Why not? It was his friend. Only to my surprise his friend was really trying to get in my pants. This did not flush with me, and I dropped him off quick.

I went to a girlfriend's house. We all decided to have a few drinks and before I knew it, it was 3:00 am in the morning. So, I left their house and went to my apartment, really drunk by now. I probably was there about fifteen minutes when I heard CA pull up. I jumped in bed and acted like I was asleep. He entered my bedroom because he had a key to my apartment. He snatched the covers off and said, "Don't act like you've been here all-night sleeping."

I said, "I have."

"There's no way; the hood on your car is still hot."

Well, I guess that was a lie. Anyway, I did not want to have sex because I was just too drunk to maintain but I guess that was not a question if I did. That was the night I got pregnant again for the third and last time. I did not know it then, but I would soon find out. Remember I am the one that is highly drunk with no control, so I guess I was to blame for that. And, sure enough, later I did get blamed for it. It happens, right? You think if the man was on the bottom, he had the upper hand, right?

Well, it was three months later, and I was not feeling well. I was having my periods, so I just knew there was no way I was pregnant. Then I started spotting so I knew something was not right. I made an appointment with my doctor only to learn, yeah, I was pregnant. I could not understand how it happened because I was on birth control. So, I just knew he would understand and be happy that I was, only to find out he was not. We went round after round over this, but I played so I had to pay the price. I was going to be a mom again. Once again, I felt if he just gave it a try, he would become the man he needed to be. Well, I was wrong again. It seemed to push him further away.

Well, he wanted me to go with him when he went to tell his parents. I thought they might have been Ok with the idea, but I believe his father was more upset than his mom. His father began to ask so many questions at one time he had my head spinning. These were things that CA and I had not even thought about discussing yet. His father asked him if we were going to get married. I spoke up and said, "Not because of this."

His father asked him right in front of me, "Do you LOVE her?" To my surprise he could not even answer his dad. That should have been my clue, but I was only thinking about my child again growing up without a father. It was more than I wanted to accept. So, he wanted to do the right thing and marry me so our baby would have his last name. If only I could have seen in a crystal ball, I would never have married him for that reason at all. I did not know at the time that our baby could have carried his last name and I did not have to marry him.

We got married in March of 1988. We both went to the justice of the peace and said our vows. Wow, what a wedding. Anyway, I did not let that get to me. I was married, and our baby would have a father in his or her life. Trying to save money, I sold my place to move into a house his parents owned. CA continued to play music at different bars on Friday and Saturday nights.

I stopped going with him because I was gaining weight and not feeling as well as I did at the beginning of the marriage. The night I started having contractions my husband was playing at a bar in Norfolk. So, I called the bar and told the bouncer to tell him I was on the way to the hospital to have the baby. He showed up maybe a few hours later. When he arrived, the doctor was examining me, only to find out that when the baby was coming, she was going to come feet first. He informed both of us he would have to take it by the next morning if the fetus had not turned. Of course, she did not, so I was rolled into the OR to have a c-section. CA wanted a boy. To me it didn't matter, as long as the child was healthy. So, in less than ten minutes in OR she was born. My husband's reactions were not what you would want to hear as a wife. "Put it back; it was supposed to be a boy."

I was hurt but I thought he was just making a joke. Well, the next few days was a struggle trying to come up with a name for her. So, since he wanted a boy, and she was a girl I decided to come up with a name with his first two initials. So, I named her Charlotte Ann. It sounded like a sweet name, and it was part of him.

I went home with staples in my stomach from the surgery. I had decided to breast feed since I had not tried it with my boys. I guess it was something new and I thought I could handle it. Well, to my surprise it was a little rough on my body, but I tried it for six weeks. It was the most painful thing in the world to me. I could not keep them pumped fast enough. I remember the day my husband came home I begged him to do what he had to do to keep them down. He had to nurse them just like a child to help with the pain. Oh boy, it helped so much. I had to rearrange and go back to bottle feeding. Much better but some women are good with breast-feeding.

Well, I was adjusting my lifestyle to the baby's schedule and being the wife that I should be. Things just seemed so good at first. However, since I had a responsibility to stay home and take care of a child, I was not able to go with him to the bars anymore to listen to him play. It seemed as if I needed something to do, so I could get out and unwind a bit myself. So, I heard about a warehouse coming to Suffolk and they were going to be hiring. I got my babysitter that kept my son PJ for me to watch Charlotte so I could go and fill out the application and get a job. I was always a person who worked and did not mind helping. So, I thought this would take a load off my husband some as well. It was about two weeks later I got a call to go to the vocational center for an interview. So, I did, and they stated I would be called if they wanted me to come back in a few days for the second interview.

So, on a Wednesday I got another call to go back and be interviewed again. Well, to my surprise I was hired that day to start in September of 1988. I was excited and depressed at the same time. Now I knew I would have to leave my children with a sitter instead of taking care of them. However, Amelia was a great person and sitter, and I became more comfortable after talking to her.

Well, shortly after I started working, CA and I moved to outer Suffolk on College Drive. We moved because there was an issue going on between him and his father, so it was time to move out of the house they owned. We had been settled in for almost a year when I found items that led me to believe my husband was not being faithful. Also, I found out by someone else he was not; but because of the individual I swore to them I would carry it to my grave. Which I will!!!!

Prior to this they were going to have a Christmas party at his job which I was kind of looking forward to. So, I asked about it when I found the tickets in his shirt pocket. He snatched them from me and threw them in the trash can. Well, the next day I noticed the trash can had been emptied, which I found odd since normally all my husband did was carry the trash can to the street. So, after he left to go to work, I went into the garage and emptied that trash bag onto the floor to find out he had taken the tickets out. I knew then he was going to the party, but it was not going to be with me. So, I did not address it then. I waited until the day of the party to ask him what he was going to do that day and night. His response to me was nothing today, but I am going to hang out with the guys in the band and practice tonight. I went right along with it. Well, I woke up around 3:00 am that morning, and he still was not home. So, I'd already told him when I married him if I suspected he was running around on me I would end the marriage and never look back.

Well, to my surprise he showed up the next afternoon and to his surprise I had all his clothes packed and waiting for him on the sofa. Boy, did he try to justify some good lies. I could not even stand to look him in his face. He begged me to let him stay and we could work it all out. I tried but I could not stand for him to touch me. I allowed him to stay for another two weeks.

I came home one day from work, and he had left some money on the dresser in our bedroom with a letter. The letter stated he could not bear to live with us anymore knowing what he had done. It was not fair to me nor the children. So, I guess you could say that was him admitting to his guilt. I continued to live in the house for a few more months. But I had to get out of that house; it was driving me insane. I searched for an apartment and decided to move into the Dunedin apartments. They were furnished with some utilities which would help me out as far as rent. My best friend, Brenda, always told me to keep my head up and never look back. I moved out, transferred everything to the apartment, and got settled in with the children. CA paid his child support but saw Charlotte very little because of his lifestyle. It was always an excuse that amounted to my fault. However, he did not have a problem wanting to continue to sleep with me. I did this to get money for things for my children not because I enjoyed it at this point. So why continue to tell people the wrong things about why you did not see her?

I had been separated from my husband for about six months or less. I started talking to this guy on my job as well as my friend, Brenda. He would always kid around with us, and I never thought anything about it at first. Then he would tell Brenda to get me to go out with him. She told me what he said on the way home.

Brenda and I would rotate driving because we both worked the same shift. Time went by and the guy, David, ended up training Brenda and me on the forklift. I continued to chat with him and decided why not go out with him? I was still a little skeptical at first. I did not feel right since I was still legally married to my husband. However, I figured what's fair for the goose is fair for the gander.

David and I went out a few times and things seemed good. He was nice and seemed to be sincere. However, to my surprise I found out later after the fact he was seeing another person. I was told they were separated but I should have gone with my gut, and I would probably not have messed with him. Then again, I was lonely and hurt from my marriage. I guess it really did not matter at that time. I stopped seeing him because I thought if he wanted to be with me, he would come back around. If not, then he would be with the girl he was seeing.

I feel it was a challenge in my life, and the rush of it made me chase after him. So, I guess it was not meant for me to be with him. It was not long after this happened that David left the job. Well, years later he married that girl and they had a daughter together. I continued to check on his life at random times. I was a friend with one of his friends who kept me posted on his life. To my surprise I found out years later that he had divorced his wife and gotten married to someone else. I found out that he hardly got out of one marriage before he was jumping into another one. You must give yourself time to heal from the damage from one before you do it again. That I learned from the previous one myself. I had assumed he was still married to her until…

Well, at this point I decided to stay single for a while and focus on trying to buy a house. I buried myself in working a lot of overtime and focusing on my children's sports. About a year after I was in my house, I went to Lowes in Churchland to buy things I needed for the place. I had been going to Lowes for a few months when I met this guy working there. We sort of eyed each other at about the same time. Neither one of us let on but I think we both knew. Well, he helped me, and I thanked him and went on. I returned the next day for some more stuff for the house and yes, he was working again. So, this time I decided to introduce myself to him and he told me his name. He asked me if I would be interested in going out so we could get to know each other. I agreed. I gave him my number and told him to call me when he wanted to.

Jeff called me about a week later and asked me if I wanted to go to the waterfront to sit and talk. I told him I would meet him at this bar on the corner of Portsmouth Blvd. This way I could follow him to where we were going. Well, when we got there, he asked if I wanted to go in and grab a bite to eat and have a drink. I said, "Why not?" So, we did. After we finished, we decided to go ahead and make our way to the waterfront in Portsmouth. He stated it was nice and I would enjoy it. Jeff started to walk me to my car and there was an empty parking place beside my car. This car pulled up so fast beside him he was almost hit. Currently, I was already in my car with my window down talking to him. This woman jumped out of her car and asked him what he was doing. I looked at him and her and I said, "Who is this?"

She continued to tell me he was her boyfriend. I looked at Jeff and I became so angry I told him to move away from my car. He tried to explain to me they were no longer together. I didn't care; I was not going to get caught up in that drama.

Well, for the next few days Jeff continued to call until finally I answered to ask him why. He stated, "I tried to tell you I was not living with her anymore. I have a room with a friend, but you would not give me a chance."

We continued to see each other, and he bought my daughter a swing set for her birthday and put it together for her. I thought that was so sweet. He seemed to be a good man.

I came home one day to find a message on my answering machine from his ex. I could not understand how she got my number, but it was not something to worry about at that time. My friend, Brenda, was there, and we both listened to the message she had left me. This woman poured her heart out to me for about 20 minutes. It hurt me so bad to hear what she had been through with this man. I tried to sleep that night and all I could think about was how much pain this woman had on her shoulders. Jeff had been with her and helped raise her daughter. So, this child looked up to him as a father figure. It was becoming too much for me to carry on my shoulders.

I called Jeff and told him I needed to see him as soon as he could come over. He stated, "I'll be by when I get off at six."

When he got there, I think he realized something was not right. I let him listen to the message. He tried to convince me not to let that change things between us, but I just could not be the woman to come in between that. I ended our relationship and he begged me for months to give us another try. My heart would not let me.

Jeff and this girl got back together months later and had a daughter together. However, years later they separated. I know because I saw him in the mall, and he stopped me to tell me. However, at this time ten years later, I had remarried again. I regret to this day letting him go but maybe one day I will see him again. He had so many good characteristics about him that I never got to see because I let him go. Good luck, love, wherever you are.

After I stopped dating Jeff and got past the shock of things, I eventually decided it was time to try again to see if dating was an option. There was this guy that worked with me on my job. He knew I was having car problems so he told me to go to this guy named Ernie and he would help me. I asked him to find out first if I could bring it by in a few days.

He came back the next day to tell me to bring it the next day. So, Bruce showed me where his shop was, and I stopped by to get it checked out. Well, he checked it out and asked me if I could leave it for a few days and he would fix it. I asked how much it was going to cost, and he could not tell me until he found out exactly what was wrong with it. Well, the next day Ernie called me to tell me my car was ready, and I could come and pick it up. I asked how much, and he said, "I will let you know when you get here."

So, I stopped by the bank and picked up some money. Still not knowing was not helping the situation out. Well, when I arrived, he stated he had to replace some sort of switch and some other part. Since I am not mechanically knowledgeable, I said thanks. I asked him how much and he said no charge.

I did not buy that, so I insisted on paying him because I did not want it to bite me later. So, he took some money even though he didn't want to. However, I felt better. As I was leaving, he asked me if I was married and I stated no. I asked why, and he said, "Come by on Wednesday and have a cold beer." He said he usually cooks on the grill. So, what did I have to lose? He was cute with those blue eyes. Little did I know they were just as dangerous as they were alluring.

I arrived on that Wednesday at his shop and to my surprise there were a few people hanging around up there. It was mainly older fellows hanging out to shoot the breeze with each other. Somewhere for those who'd retired to hang out at. I believe he was cooking chicken for us to eat. It was a different vibe, and everyone seemed to be nice and sipping on their cold beers.

Time passed and it was getting later. I had to pick up my children, so I ended the night with a "Thank you, I enjoyed it." He walked me to my car and asked if he could see me again.

I said, "Just give me a call." So, for the next couple of months I would hang out at his shop on Wednesdays and enjoy talking to his friends. The more I got to know Ernie, I thought he was a nice guy and he seemed to be honest. So, around the 3rd month of hanging out, Ernie asked me if I wanted to go to South Carolina to the races. I was not for sure if I wanted to go or not. I told him I had to see if I could get someone to watch the children. He stated, "If you need money for a sitter, I will pay for that as well."

Boy, he was really wanting to go out of his way. I figured since I had never been, it might be fun. I planned with my sitter so I could go to the race in about two weeks. I really thought, "Man, this will be a great time and to be sure it is going to be fun.

Well, it was two weeks later, and I was headed to South Carolina with Ernie in his bright red Ford truck. I was so excited; what a getaway. I had not had one of them in a while and I was overwhelmed by the road trip there. The view of things and the conversation was great as well. We checked into the hotel where he had planned to stay. On the way back to the room we decided to stop by the ABC store and pick up some alcohol. Of course, it was my choice, and I chose Absolut. We walked later around the area sipping on our drinks and talking about a lot of things. Ernie mentioned to me, "Let's go and get something to eat."

We showed up at a restaurant and to my surprise I had to tell him we needed to leave. I had drunk more than I realized, and the room was spinning. It was hard trying to play like everything was okay when it was not. He took me back to the room so I could calm down some. I was a little upset and torn up by now. Even though I was the way I was, he tried to get me to settle down. Evening had fallen and before we knew it, it was getting late.

I was hoping he would go to bed and just not make a pass at me. It did not happen that way and things got a little heated up. I tried to tell him I really was not ready for this in my life yet. I became very angry at him at first but then I just gave up and gave in. I was mad at myself, but he was kind and understanding and took his time with me which made the whole situation much better. It was a nice night. Well, the next morning was not such a good morning. I had a hangover–something I had not suffered in a long time. It was going to be about 90 degrees that day and my head was pumping and hurting. He stopped by the store and got me something for my headache. However, it did not do a thing for my stomach. I felt like I was going to throw up any minute. He laughed at me all day. Glad he saw the humor; I sure did not.

Off to the race we went. We entered the racetrack grandstands, and I just knew before I got to the seat, I would not make it. I think I might have sat there for thirty minutes, max. I told him I had to go back to the truck and get some air. The heat was just too much for my head and stomach to bear. He was upset with me because then I had to hear about how much those tickets cost. At that point I didn't care if they cost two hundred dollars. Before I got back to the truck I threw up until I just felt like I was going to pass out. That's what I got for drinking too much. Anyway, I turned on the AC in his truck and stayed there until he came back out from the race. I probably slept for two hours. I looked as if I had been sleeping for days. I needed that in more ways than one. When he returned, he was still angry at me, but he ended up apologizing because if he had not bought it, I would not have drunk it, right? Well, the day seemed as though it would never end. As the sun finally set, I was able to eat something, so I started to feel better. We decided to stay one more night before heading back home.

Well, as some say, all good things come to an end. I was back at home from the trip to South Carolina and life was good. Ernie and I continued to see each other. After around ten months of seeing him, I found out he was still married and living with his wife. I could not believe this. How could a man pull this off, stay nights with me on the weekend and be married? I was angry with him, and I did not even want to talk to him.

Finally, he tracked me down to talk to me about it. He stated he did live with her for the children's sake, but they were done. I told him I would not deal with situations like this. What was he teaching his children? Well, we continued to talk to each other until he finally said, "How about if I move in with you? I was not sure at first because my children had never seen me with anybody, and I did not know how that would go. I talked to PJ and Charlotte about it, and they were happy if I was. So, I agreed to it, and we continued to live together for about two years and so many months. Things seemed as though something was just not right. He started to show signs as if he were up to no good. I just let it go for a while until he started not coming home at night. When I questioned him, it was always an excuse of staying with his children at their grandma's house. So, as I became more suspicious of his action, I started to ask questions. As he gave me the answers I started to document. Then I asked a few individuals I knew to check out where he stated he was staying. The place did not even exist.

I had an event coming up for my job that he told me he would take me to. I decided after that I was going to get to the bottom of this. So, Ernie took me on my cruise that Saturday and stayed at my house that night. He was trying to reel me in enough so I would not question things anymore. However, that was the wrong answer for me.

I did more digging only to find out he had moved in with some other woman. I was so hurt and upset all at the same time. I went to his shop to confront him only for him to tell even more lies. After I found out who the person was, I called her father to tell them about Ernie. The answer that her father gave me really blew my mind. Her father told me that I was caught in a love triangle because Ernie had been an honest man to his daughter, and they were getting ready to get married. You know what? I could not believe he wouldn't even listen.

I could have showed him the picture of where we had gone on the Spirit of Norfolk that weekend, but it was not even worth trying. I decided to let Karma take care of him. I can remember when I first started to deal with him in a relationship. I always told him, "If you decide to be involved with someone else just tell me." Really, how hard was that to just be honest!! You try not to wish anyone bad luck and I tried to see the lesson I learned from the breakup. To my surprise six months later Ernie had a heart attack. The person I am I still called to check on him to make sure he was ok. He could not believe I called. What he said to me really floored me. His words to me were, "I guess you wished I would have died so you could have spit on my grave." I could not believe he said that. My response was, "Ernie, you did not even learn nothing about the person you lived with. My heart is something I wear on my sleeve."

He stopped and thought for a minute and said, "You are so right."

I know in my heart if I needed something from him now, he would be there for me. Thanks, Ernie, for teaching me a good lesson.

It probably was around 1992 or 1993, I received a phone call that would change my whole life in a different direction. The person on the other end of the phone identified himself as Billy and told me he was the man that had been raising my son. At first, I thought someone was playing a joke on me and I became very upset until he told me my sons' real name. Then I knew it had to be my boy.

He talked to me for about ten to fifteen minutes to let me know that DJ wanted to meet me. I was excited and scared at first over the whole thing. I started having flashbacks of my previous life and did not even know which way I should go first. I did not know where to begin really. I knew there were a lot of things that I'd have to do on my end. I had a son, PJ, that was his real brother that I had not even told him about. I didn't know how he was going to react to the whole story. I was not sure if he was going to be mad at me since I had not told him all these years. So, I called PJ who was at one of his friend's houses playing and I asked him to come back home. Of course, being a child, he wanted to know why. I told him I had to talk to him at home. So, he was there in about fifteen minutes. It was the hardest thing I had to do, and it took me thirty minutes to finally get it together to tell him. He looked at me and said, "Really, Mom? I want to see him."

I had to explain the whole thing to him so he would understand that it would be a process. So, Billy made the arrangements in the next few weeks for us to meet at Sleepy Hole Park. However, he stated if it rained, he would have us to meet at a hotel. Well, good news…it did not rain, and we met at the park. They wanted me to meet him first, so I agreed. It was like I had a honk of cold in my throat. I did not know what to expect. When we met eye to eye neither one of us could say anything at first. I knew he was just as scared as I. Well, Billy and Rose knew he was not going to talk while they were standing around, so they walked away. I was glad because I was already nervous enough and did not need the extra pressure. After they left, DJ began to ask me a lot of questions about his biological father. They did not want me to tell him that he was locked up, but I did not want to start the relationship off in a lie either. So, when he asked, I told him he was in jail. I told him he had a real brother and a stepsister. He wanted to know a lot about them both especially knowing he had a brother. He asked if his biological father was ever in his life. I told him no, he was not. It was just the three of us.

I showed him pictures of them, and he wanted to meet them. I told him that would have to be up to his parents now. So, I tried to explain how all the years that had gone by that I still knew where he was, but I could not come near him for the fear of going to jail. I never stopped loving him and would never do so. I told him to talk to Billy and Rose and I would let him see his siblings. About two weeks went by and DJ showed up one night without them knowing he was coming. I told him I would not lie to them if they called. I wanted to do it the right way. Would they let DJ come and stay at my house overnight? But they decided for PJ to come and stay with him. PJ was so excited and yet I was nervous about all of it.

Well, I let him go and the two of them have not been separated from each other since that day. They may live separate lives, but they keep up with each other. His stepsister Charlotte always wanted to hang with them, but her age difference just did not work. However, she loved them both dearly. It was such a delight to me to know that I was able to see my birth son after all those years. It was a happy and crying moment that no one will ever fully understand unless you lived through it. Brandon is now called DJ. His name was changed to protect him down the road because he was adopted in the same city and state which is not a normal process. I was so glad it happened that way. Thanks to Rose.

The two boys hung out a lot once everyone was ok with the situation. DJ decided to go into the Marines and had been in for a year or so. When he came home, he convinced his brother to join as well. To my surprise he enlisted and was off to Parris Island. I was not for sure I agreed with both joining up, but it was their life, and I could not live it for them. It was tough on their sister because they both were not around. She was always closer to her brother PJ because he was more like a father figure to her. Her brother DJ was the one that was more laid back as she is. Her love for them is the same though.

After my breakup, after almost a year, I decided that since my daughter was becoming a teenager, I did not want to stay in the city anymore. I was going to move to the country. I felt like the city moved at a much faster pace. Little did I even suspect that I should have stayed where I was.

I rode around for weeks until I found this house on Desert Road on the Carolina side that was for sale. I took the information down and called about it on Monday morning. It was in my price range, and I asked to see the inside of it. I was amazed; I bought it. The individuals that owned it had smoked; however, I loved the layout. So, I had to put mine up for sale with the option that they had to give me 60 days before I had to get out. I already knew I was approved for the house—just a matter of selling mine. It worked out to the good. I began packing and the children were excited and upset at the same time. They were going to be leaving their friends. I understood that but I just needed to enjoy a new beginning for us all.

Well, everything was looking good. Each of us was getting settled into our new home in North Carolina. It was nice. I had a lot of room outside and a nice sized garage. We really did not need four bedrooms, but it was nice to have a spare for guests. I worked on it a little at a time until I had the inside smelling nice and no more smoke smell.

I really enjoyed working on my yard getting flowers planted and trellises put in place. It was a process because it was now just me and the children. Things were so hard sometimes not having a male around to help. The boys were living their own lives, so I only saw them from time to time. You had to catch them in between dodging everyone else.

My friend, Margie, who lived in Carolina decided to introduce me to one of her husband's friends. So, she called me up and asked me to come to a cookout. I prepared something to take and went. It was a blind meeting so that was a little outside of my normal routine of meeting someone. However, I trusted my friend in her choice. She set it up so no one knew anything about the other one. This way if either he or I did not see the connection then nothing was lost. So, when I arrived, he was already there with his two sons. Margie introduced me to Alan. We spoke and kept it simple while continuing to converse with others at the cookout. His sons Jessie and Johnny asked me if I had any children and their names. When I told them, I had a daughter at Gates they both stood at attention. They both knew her and thought she was cute. Anyway, as the night was ending, and I had to go Alan walked me to the car to see if he could get my number. So, I wrote it down for him and told him to enjoy the rest of the night. I wasn't for sure if he was really my type. So, about a week went by and he called and wanted to know if I would like to go to Nags Head with him for a few days.

My response was, "No, I do not know you that well to spend nights with you, especially in a hotel."

He reassured me that he would get a room with two beds in it. Really that was supposed to make me feel better. So, I told him I would get with him in a few days and let him know. As soon as I hung up talking with him, I called my friend to ask her if she thought it would be a safe thing to do. She said, "Yes, Wanda, he will be a perfect gentleman."

I called him back two days later and laid out my ground rules and he was good with that.

Well, the next week I had to get a sitter to watch out for Charlotte so I could make the journey. I remember when he pulled up, he was driving a Mustang which I thought was nice. When we left my yard, I made a comment about how nice the car was only to find out it belonged to one of his sons. He stated he had a vehicle but thought the car would be better. I agreed it was. On the way, we went to the beach. When we arrived at the hotel it was nice, and it did have two separate beds which was a plus and he did do what he said he would. So, we unpacked the car and he said, "Let's go get something to eat. We went to a sea-food place on the main highway which was very nice and so relaxing. We stayed there for a few hours talking and laughing about different things. Basically, getting to know each other.

Then we went back to the hotel and got us a mixed drink and headed down to the water. It was so nice; the breeze was cool and calm. The ocean waves were breaking on shore, but the ocean was calm, not angry. We took our chairs down to the water and relaxed even more with the water flowing through our toes. As the sun started to go down and the moon shone across the water it was breathtaking. Well, so much for that day. It was time to resign to the room. We stayed up late talking and asking each other questions. Well, it was late now, and it was time to call it a night. The night ended well and both of us went out as soon as our heads hit the pillow.

Day two we woke up to a beautiful sunrise across the ocean. I had a coffee mug in my hand and the mixed fragrance of the ocean and rich coffee. What a way to wake up! It was like something out of a magazine. Alan suggested we go and have breakfast; then we could hang out on the beach the rest of the day. So, we did and came back and grabbed the cooler filled with cold beer. With a blanket in hand and a few towels we were off to the beach. It was probably about eighty-five degrees that day. It was such a beautiful sunny day. Not too hot and not too cool!! I sat in the beach chairs and indulged in some ice-cold beers for the next three hours. Alan talked and told me about his life before me and I sort of briefed him on some of mine. I really did not know where the RELATIONSHIP was going so why tell everything? We decided to call it an early night because we were going to leave in the morning. And yes, being a man, he sure tried to get me to let him sleep with me that night. "No," I told him, "You do not know me, and I sure do not know enough about you."

Well, we hit the sack. The morning seemed to come too early, and the good time was over. So, on the way back to my house Alan asked me if he could see me again and I agreed.

Well, for the next few weeks Alan and I started seeing each other more and more each week. Either I would come to his house, or he would come to mine. We started having get togethers at my house with his family and mine about a year after first seeing each other. Alan moved in with me and we decided to sell his house in Boone Town and take the money from his house to put a garage up in the back yard. I really thought if we had just added on the one that was there it would have been better. Alan was not a man who worked on cars or used a garage a whole lot. However, it was his money, so I had no problem if that's what he wanted to do. Before he could sell his house, he learned he would get more money for it if he had a permanent foundation. So, I helped him to get it done. I felt since he was increasing the value of my place it was the right thing to do. However, he was dealing with an ex-wife that he had been separated from for a couple of years. I felt he should divorce her so if something happened, I would not be screwed out of the money with which I was helping him. So, Alan's ex filed the papers and about nine months later we got married on July 7th. I look back on the situation and it should have been done differently, but I could not see her get what was his because she was the one that was wrong in the marriage is what I was told. Years to come I would see things a little different, however.

Well, we got married if you call a marriage going to the justice of the peace, saying your vows, then going back to work. It was not what I dreamed a wedding should be like. His son and my daughter were our witnesses. I wanted friends and family involved in the wedding, but I guess it was what it was. I thought it would be okay. Maybe a few years down the road we could have the wedding I had always wanted. That wedding consisted of being proposed to in a sleigh or a carriage driven by horses. I just have always thought a wedding with snow was the most romantic thing in the world. So much for wishful thinking. It is still my dream engagement one day, if not in this life, the one after.

As the two of us watched our children grow up in front of our eyes there were some days that were not so good. One thing I can say for Alan and me, we both tried our best to treat the children equally. It was tough at times, especially for the last two. Johnny and Charlotte both had their own minds and ways of looking at things.

Charlotte was spoiled because of being the girl. Still, it was no excuse. I should have not given in as much as I did to her. Charlotte began hanging out with the wrong people and she took a turn for the worse in the drug world. She became pregnant at the age of 17 with this guy she had been seeing named Thomas. I was so upset with her. I had talked so much to her about having sex and being careful. SO much for a motherly talk. I went to the home of his parents to see what they were going to do to support this matter. Charlotte had one more year of school and I wanted her to at least graduate. So, at the time I worked Wednesday through Saturday. I requested they watch the baby on the days Charlotte went to school. We all agreed on this so she could finish school. However, we knew she would be out for the six weeks once the baby was born. Well, here we go.

On December 27, 2007, I took Charlotte to the doctor because she was having pains in her back. The baby was supposed to be born in February. However, they had another plan for all of us. After the doctor examined Charlotte, she told me to go ahead and take her to the hospital because this baby was coming today. So off to the hospital we went to get Charlotte checked in. It was a long day but finally here came the baby girl. Charlotte and Thomas named her Haley. Haley was a tiny little thing, but she was so cute. Well, nice after-Christmas gift. Everyone was tired so we all went home to get some rest.

Charlotte and the baby came home the next day. It was a life change for all of us at the house. Having a newborn to take care of in our home was now a challenge. Of course, Alan and I had already raised our children, so we thought those days were over. Little did we know it was just beginning. Charlotte became depressed about things because Haley's father decided not to be with her anymore. I guess he was young and as scared as she was. So, a lot of the responsibility fell on Alan and me. Alan was a great man as far as things with our children. He was a great person to my children as well.

Our relationship was a different issue. You know they say individuals change after you get married; that is so true. In my case I was the same person he knew from the beginning. Alan was a man who made sure he went to work every day no matter if he was sick or not. That I can be very blessed for. However, when it came to helping with things around the house or in the house that was something for which he had no energy. I guess as a wife I picked up a lot of the slack and made things happen when they needed to. As time passed Haley became about three, I will say. Charlotte got involved with debts and drinking and Thomas stepped in and took custody of Haley. Charlotte could not see what she was doing wrong, and Alan and I had to just let it go. We hoped she would learn on her own.

In the next few years, Alan lost his job after being at the mill for thirty-three years. Before they let him go, we had discussed getting a vending trailer so he could do that after he left the mill. He was going to get a package deal and he would use the money to buy that. I thought it would be a great idea for him and someone else to do as a seasonal thing. So, I went and had some business cards and I made flyers up and booked events for him. In the meantime, I went online and applied for a part time job at Lowes. I really did not think I was going to get a call, but they called back very soon for an interview. I was not sure I wanted to do that, but I felt as his wife I could help do my part. Boy, my mom was upset with me for taking on a second job. I knew she was right but by this time I just needed to get away from all the issues going on in the house. I thought it would be good for me as well as my married life. I felt like I was being pulled in so many directions and did not know which was up or down. After I started working at Lowes it helped to separate from all the hustle and bustle, so I felt like I had some sort of life again (even though that was not the case). After I started to work for Lowes and got to know my co-workers, I found myself talking to a lady named Linda. I really enjoyed our talks, and I became very close to her. She would always listen to me and give me the greatest advice on all my issues, whether it was at home or on the job. Linda and I became very close through the whole time I worked there. She is a great person and a wonderful friend. She will always be there for me through thick and thin. Thanks, Linda, for all your support. We keep up with each other even today.

Well, Alan's trailer business was taking off and I had to help him with that as well. So, I was now helping as a grandma, stepmom, wife, home, Lowes employee, and helping Alan run his trailer which was supposed to be for him and someone else to do. I was just about ready to leave and never be found. How much does someone think one person can take? I did it until I just could not deal with Alan being lazy about things, and I believe he became depressed because of the loss of his job. However, he just left everything up to me to do. I thought a marriage was supposed to be fifty-fifty. I started to work more hours at Lowes and stayed away from home as much as I could. Was that the answer? Probably not but it seemed to ease the stress a bit for a while.

It appears things were becoming more difficult at home and the finances were out of control. I kept taking money out of my savings to pay for the mortgage to save my home. It just seemed as though it was not helping. I can remember when I asked my husband to check on his retirement to help save the home his words were, "It is not open for discussion."

That is when I realized how little he cared. Things just kept spiraling out of control, and I knew the marriage was heading down a not-so-good road. So, I told him we just needed to sell the house and he go his way and I go mine. So, at this point in the marriage I had decided not to get another penny out of my savings to save the house. I had this home before I ever knew Alan so to lose something I had before I married him, it really hurt bad. So, I had to work hard the next three months to get things packed to move.

I went to an apartment building in Suffolk and inquired about the cost. I rented a three bedroom with two baths. I needed a room for Charlotte and Memphis. Charlotte had gotten involved with someone else and became pregnant again. Memphis was born in Greenville. So, it was now the three of us. Charlotte, of course, was not working yet so she was able to stay home with Memphis for a while. I was still working two jobs and helping with Memphis. Memphis was a joy in my life just like all my grandchildren have been. However, when they live with you, they become even more special. It is not because the love is any different because I love them all the same.

I was hoping that Charlotte had her life together this time and could do right by her son. We'd been living on our own for about eight months and I decided to give my marriage another try. Alan came and moved in with us and to my surprise he still had not changed on some things. He did have a job working with a construction company which only lasted for a little while. He said they laid him off. Well, he got another job about a month later.

I tried for about a year and I decided I could not live with him anymore. It just did not seem as though he was trying as hard as I was. No matter what I did, it was just not good enough. Anyway, I called my mom and asked her if I could move in there so I could save up some money. I had never lived with my mom ever since I was on my own at eighteen. She allowed us to stay until Charlotte went back to her old ways. So, then my mom and I decided to go after custody when she left Memphis and stayed gone.

Nana and GG now have full custody of Memphis and he resides with Nana in Suffolk. His Mom is still locked up but should be able to come home in January 2021. Memphis and I are hoping and praying that Charlotte will get her life back on track and be the BEST mom from here on out. Time will tell it all and we can only wish her the best of luck.

Alan went to live with his mom in North Carolina and we still communicate because of Memphis. Alan has always been in his life, and he calls him his POPOP. I would never take that from him in this life and wish nothing but the best for Alan in his life. We both left on good terms and have no problem helping the other person if they need something within reason. Good luck, ALAN!!!

Alan and I had been separated for almost two years and I continued to work for Lowes until August 2018. I realized I needed to stop to take care of Memphis. I worked two jobs for almost ten years. I did this so I could buy me another house so I would have somewhere for us. Thanks to my mom for supporting me those years with Memphis and supporting me on buying my house in 2017. It was a great moment to watch it being built for Memphis and me. We moved in two weeks before Christmas in 2017. It was a very stressful time, but I wanted him to have his first Christmas in the new house. Things have been good for us both and he sticks right with his Nana wherever she goes. His love for his GG is unconditional as well as her love for him. Memphis has always been around adults and will talk to you like one. So, I decided he needed to be around other children and to a babysitter he went. It has done him good to be with other children. However, it was time for Nana to try to get out and mingle some with other folks. Talking to a 5-year-old all the time is nice but adult time was needed.

On March 2019 Memphis and I were in Food Lion picking up some groceries. I happened to notice someone was looking at me and I was trying to figure out who it was. They were a little far away from me, so it was hard to tell who it was. As he got closer, I realized it was a friend of mine from the past: David. We spoke to each other for a few minutes, and I asked him how he was doing and told him to stop by the house sometime. He tried to give me his number, but I said I could get it from his friend that I knew. So, off to the checkout line Memphis and I went. When I got home, I thought about whether I should call him or not. I know we both were young back in the past; however, I just did not know. I have always cared a lot about him—just did not know if I was ready for memory lane again. I waited about two weeks and on March 23, 2019 I decided to text him. He responded back which surprised me. I knew David had gotten married again and I did not know where he was in his life. So, I took a chance and invited him to stop by on the weekend. He stopped by on a Friday night, and we drank a few beers and talked.

After a few times of stopping by, I asked him where he was in his life, and he had just gotten out of a relationship with some girl that I think lasted three months. He stated he was still legally married to his wife of ten years. I am not sure how long he was away from his wife before he got involved with the other lady. Really had not asked him that question yet. He had three dogs that he thought a lot about that were staying in a house with his ex. They were destroyed in a house fire. David was so hurt by this that it took a toll on him. They were part of his family and he blamed himself because of how things unfolded in his marriage.

Life is unfair to all of us, but we can never predict how things will turn out. David has always been honest with me in sharing things about his life. We had been hanging out for about three months now and there were times things got heated up. I was not sure I wanted to put myself in that situation again, especially knowing he was not looking for a commitment now. I guess I just let myself become weak and gave in. Making love to someone always put things on a different avenue. However, I had to realize what I had put myself into. At this point I still was not sure I did the right thing for me. I knew things would not be easy, but I guess I was willing to give it a try.

David has a side about him that I have come to enjoy and like about him. He takes his time with me in all things. Something that is important in any relationship, friend or not. Plus, I have always thought about him and cared for him. I just figured I could be his friend and not let my heart get involved. By December it was becoming tough, but I stayed the same as always. Your heart is not something you can turn on and off like a light switch. I enjoy talking and laughing with him. We talk about a lot of things. Probably things most people cannot even talk about in a relationship. We enjoy each other's company.

Well, on January 3, 2020, David lost his father who had been living with him for over a year. This only added to this year's grief, because it it was the same day last year that he lost his dogs. So, to deal with another tragedy on that date was hard. I received a call on my job from his aunt telling me about it, so I was on the way out the door when his friend called me and asked me not to come. His friend Lee told me that his wife (EX) was already there, and it was best for me not to come. I was truly hurt to know I could not be there for him, but I had to accept it for the face value it was. She was still his wife in the eyes of the law. David did not need the pressure of having to deal with it and trying to deal with calling everyone. Days went by and he became distant to me, and I could not understand why. I really wanted to be there for my friend. I went by and dropped off some food for the family and left to keep peace. I was able to meet the other aunt that I did not know. However, I have always known two of his aunts. So, I left things alone until everyone returned home and life moved back on track for David. My two friends at my work–Joyce and Iris–have been my rock in this situation. Joyce always told me I deserved better than this, because "David does not know the person he has standing in front of him."

I sent a letter to his house letting him know how he made me feel through the whole process of what he had done to me. Here is what the letter said in so many words. I told him how he made me feel as a friend. You do not turn your back on people who will always be there for you as if they are nothing. At this point it did not matter to me what the outcome was. I knew in my heart I had done the right thing by him as his friend. So, I also told him he needed to stop hurting women in his life. Sometimes men do not see things the way we do. But one thing for sure, they have a heart just like we do. Question ladies or gents: How can you not have feelings for someone you see day in and out for over a year and lose that affection within days. I do not think anyone can answer that without admitting feelings are involved. I tried to keep my heart out of this, but I could not. Anyway, David received the letter and we talked on the weekend after Valentine's Day. David agreed that everything I had put in that letter was correct. At first, he disagreed on one thing but when I explained it, he agreed.

Love is something you just cannot turn on and off whenever someone wants you to. So, this is when I came to realize that David had never really been in love with someone like me. He had always jumped from one extreme to the next, never giving himself a chance to heal from all the wrong in his life, whether it was his fault or not. This was the point in my life with him that I realized there were two reasons why he could not commit to anyone. First, he is still married and has not even applied for his divorce. He stated he filed for separation. I do not know for sure. I trust him that he would not outright lie about it. Second, he was still jumping from one thing to another. He told me that is why we could only be friends. It took me a few moments to take all this in and realize that maybe I could never be any more than that to him. So, I accepted it and moved on with our friendship.

On June 15th, which is my birthday, David bought a dozen red roses for me. It really took me by surprise. I could not believe it at first. I was so excited at that point I could not stand myself. All night long all I could think of was that maybe he'd had a change of heart. It was like a dream come true. Things just seemed like all was good.

I thought by now he would ask me to go to dinner or somewhere just to get out, only to find out he could not understand what was wrong with me. To my surprise he told me he did not know that colored roses meant different things. I was floored, after all my conversations with him about roses, he did not remember. I always told him do not ever give me roses unless you mean it. He looked me in my face and told me again. "I told you I did not want a relationship and that has not changed."

At that point I was so angry and hurt the only way I could deal with it was to ask him to leave. I had to have some alone time to absorb what just happened. I had to realize I could not be totally mad with him because he had been honest about not being in a relationship. This is when I truly realized what I was to David. It has now been one year, and six months and I am still hanging in there as his friend with benefits. I know I deserve better than that with him or any other man. He is still as married as he was when I met him.

As a woman, I felt in my heart that David would by now decide on really what he wants from me. I guess in my heart I probably knew all along. I thought if he saw the person, I was inside as well as outside, he would like me for who I was.

I do not think that David ever really listened to what his dad was trying to tell him at all. The dreams that he keeps having about his father are telling him something in so many ways. I get it!!! Since all this has happened and I now see what he is all about, it has never been about who I am but about him. You know I guess from being his TRUE friend I learned a lot about him as a person. He is dealing with his own demon's day in and day out. You either must let them go or continue to deal with the pain and the hurt that is tied to that. He stated he would never get back with his wife. However, as a woman in my shoes, you must wonder how much of that is true. You will understand that more once you read the next paragraph.

About a month ago I got a phone call from a Man I knew. He did not want to hurt me, and it came up on my phone as a restricted number stating he needed to tell me something about someone I was seeing. When I informed him, I was not dating anyone, he said, "Yes you are" and called out his full name to me.

At first, I started to hang up but being curious I had to listen. At first, I did not know if I really wanted to hear but I knew I had to know. He told me that David was not going to divorce his wife because she had a hold on him. He also stated he had been giving his wife money. Then he went into telling me that they have lunch together as well. Also, his truck had been seen at her house. I questioned where his wife lived to see if they knew what they were talking about and they did. It was tough trying to wrap all this around my head. Especially since a week before I left to go to Nags Head, I had asked him if he was giving her money or did, they have a loan in their names together. He said no!

Now it was like I'd been hit by a ton of bricks. How could my friend that I trusted lie to me about this? Do I believe it? With all this coming at me I had to stop and think do I have a right to question him with this at all. Yes, I do because I am sleeping with him. I do have values for myself even though I know it is wrong to be doing that since he is still legally married to his wife but legally separated. However, no matter what, the situation is a friendship and that should not ever be stomped on, and this has hurt me to the point of no return. All I want is to see him happy even if that does not include me in his life. I have come to realize that if something is worth having or wanting it is best to sit back and wait on it. Set it free and if it is meant to be it will, if not then it was not meant for you. I will end this story for now and I plan on writing another book to reveal what God has planned for me next. Whether it is with David whom I care about or someone else....

Well, since I decided to continue to write on, here we go. Well, it seemed as though the person who you thought was a friend to you turns out to be not-so-friendly. The whole time in this so-called friend-ship-with-benefits relationship, we both told each other to be honest about things. If I wanted to be with someone else or did not want to be with the other person any longer just tell the other one.

Well, I learned that the person whom I called my friend turned out not to be that person. It appears he could not be honest at all. Instead of just telling someone you are not interested in them you just throw them to the curb as though they did not even exist. I thought if you were a friend, you could be open and honest. It was not about if he wanted to be with another person. It was about showing me I was a friend to him. If he did not see the friend, I was, then he will never see anything else good in anyone. He never would allow me to be around his friends or the other side of his family. So, if I am not good enough to be around his friends then I am not good enough to be around him anymore. As Sarah Evans put it in Better Off. I want him to give me a 100 percent. However, it still hurts to know that he could be so cruel to an individual that has never hurt him in any way. Well Ladies, as the word goes, Karma will get you.

Since I wrote the above paragraph, I met with David to let him know that there was no reason he had to lie to someone who was supposed to be his friend. It is not like I haven't known him for over 30 years of my life. It was a shock to find out I did not really know that an individual could be that cruel to a good person. The reason he gave in telling a lie did not even make sense to me. Then he tells me his ex-wife has decided to file for their divorce. Well, maybe now he can be sincere when he gets involved with the next person. However, the whole time he tries to make this situation about sex and him telling me over again about not wanting a relationship. The whole time all I tried to do is tell him that it was never about that; it was just about being HONEST. I had already accepted that he would never care about me the way I did him. His response to me is that you cannot say that. I am not just at that point in my life right now. He was given almost two years with me and still nowhere. I guess I really know what I was to him. He never realized the person with whom he spent all this time. Yes, it hurt me because I have been so honest and straightforward with him. I would never lie to him nor do anything to hurt him. I have forgiven him for what he did. Deep down inside I feel there has been someone else. However, at this point I do not want to know. Who tells a person you do not want any company, yet you went off with someone? Well, I learned a lot from him. Stay away from MEN like him and never be a friend with benefits. If you cannot be number one to a person do not settle for second best.

Well, it has been two weeks now and when David left, he stated he still wanted to be able to stop by and HANG OUT WITH ME. Does he think that this won't hurt either? Really. Sometimes I feel like I am just a door mat.

Well, it is getting near time for me to decide if I am going to make my trip to Alabama to see Barbara and Jaci. I have decided that I was going with or without David at this point in my life. As the time gets near, I text Barbara to let her know I will be taking a flight out on that Sunday and renting a car at the airport. I just knew they would call David and tell him I was coming.

Well, I decided it was the right thing to do to text David and let him know I was and to see if he was still going. He texted back to ask me if he could stop by and talk. I said that was fine. I guess he was surprised that I would ask him if he still wanted to go. He said he thought I would never speak to him again. I guess David saw the other side of me. The forgiving sides! I am not saying that it did not hurt me because of what he did, but I believe in not holding grudges toward anyone. How can you heal if you dont forgive the person you care about sincerely? I hope that now David understands that it is better to tell the truth than to lie to someone who cares. Just be yourself and be true to all. It will carry you further in life. Well, we are going together to Alabama and leaving Saturday. Here we go.

Will our journey begin on a Saturday afternoon around 4:15 pm? I arrived at David's house to pick him up. It would now be him driving because he would rather drive than ride. So off to Alabama we go. We decided that we would drive for about five to six hours, then stop over for the night. Since he was driving, I did not want him to become tired and not be able to enjoy his family when he arrived the next day.

We stopped at a hotel in Georgia for the night. We chatted and talked for a few then we both jumped in the shower and ended the night making love. It was a nice evening and a peaceful night to rest. We are now back on the road at 8:15 am. We arrived in Genova around 3:00 pm that day. It was a nice roadside trip to enjoy all the things I had not seen before. Geneva is a little town. It is a peaceful place to visit and so relaxing. Barbara and Jaci made me feel right at home. I was not sure how the week would be, going somewhere with David for a week. Is it what I expected? Well, not really. The company at his aunt's was great.

I guess what really got to me about the whole trip was when his relatives came over to see him. Instead of David introducing me, he would leave that up to his aunt. Why could the man you just rode over 400 miles and slept with the night before act like you are a nobody. I felt like he did not want anyone to know I was with him. Maybe that was not the case but if it had been me with my aunts, I would have introduced him as my friend from Virginia. I guess there are a lot of things different with us as far as it goes. Well, the week went well as I expected. We visited a few historic places in Geneva that I felt were so nice. The area was like a peaceful area to just go to and read a book or be by yourself. They were decorating it for Christmas.

Well, David and I are back from Genova and the only time I have spoken to him is when he came by that Monday to pick up an Angel, I told him he could have for his tree. Other than that, we have not seen or talked to each other. I guess I put myself in the situation that I am in now. I never wanted my heart to get involved, but it did. So now I am going down the road of recovery. I started seeing a counselor to get me through this and she has helped me a lot. Everything that I have documented in this book have been things she has told me as well. So, I know I am on the way to recovery with this. David and I are very much different in a lot of ways, but I think I understand him much better than he gives me credit for. I feel we both have been through a lot of unnecessary relationships and been hurt to the extent that it causes us to think about things twice. I know as well as he does that, we will be there for each other if one needs anything.

It has been several weeks, and I stayed away from contacting him. I guess I wanted him to see me as someone with whom he would like to spend his life. I guess that would be wanting something right now and then. But staying away and not calling made him come by to see why I had not contacted him. I guess relationships can be so complicated. However, he is making me realize that we all must take it slow. Our situation is still the same. We are friends and we continue to talk to each other and hang out. We do not text every day or David does not come by like he used too. I am still not sure if this will ever become more than it is now. David has finally gotten his divorce on January 26,2021. He is glad that it is behind him so he can move on without that being a downfall in his life.

He is still dealing with the loss of his dad because he wants to redo the house that the two of them lived in together. He is not sure because he does not want his dad to think he is pushing the memories of him out the door. We talk about a lot of things; we do things together. However, I just seem to wonder why he has not introduced me to his mom or his daughter. I have not even been introduced to his best friend either. I just want to understand why. I do not know if I will ever have the answer but in due time, I will figure it all out. So, I decided to write a wish List for him, to see if he would honor any of the things that I would like for him to do. I do not feel like this is something I have to do for a man because I feel that if they care enough, it should come naturally. However, a few of my male friends informed me that some of us must be led by the hand on things. So, then I added six questions on the back that I wanted him to answer for me. I did this on the 10th of March. Still no response. I guess I will really know soon. However, one of my male friends told me that I just need to wash my hands of David because he is nothing but a player. You know I feel like that. David's life has never been about good women in his life but a lot of bar and party women. So, to have a good woman like me in his life is a very different change for him.

At this point I've put two years into this friendship or whatever it is at this point. I am not ready to throw in the towel yet. It is time for me to sit back analyze my life to see if this is what I want for another two years. I realize he needs time for himself, but he has had that. He has made no commitment to me and has lived his life as he has wanted to.

In the meantime, I have been talking to someone who knew me from high school. I met him through his aunt because we were chatting, so I guess he knew about me. I started texting him and talking to him about different things in my life as well and he did the same. I went by to see him and to talk to him only to learn he was confined to a bed and wheelchair. At first, I did not know how to take the situation but the more I talked to him the more I realized he just needed a friend. He explained to me the disease he has will eventually reach a point in which he will lose all muscle control of his body. He is being fed through a tube to survive. This is something I was not really prepared for, but I handled it very well. He can talk some, but he must communicate to me by using a computer, using his glasses to type what he wants to say to you. I am still not sure yet why he is in my life but as time goes on, I will find out.

Bill has been a true friend in answering any question I ask him about my friend. Sometimes it is a good idea to have someone else's point of view on life who does not even know anything about you. He has been the second man in my life as a friend that told me David does not realize what type of woman he has in his life. Do not get me wrong. I don't talk about things in my life about David with him I just throw a statement out and see what results I will get from it. It appears I am the one who needs to look at things differently. So, for two different men to say the same thing must mean I am a great person. Well, at this point I must realize what is meant to be. I will continue to be Bill's friend to the end. Thanks, Bill, for being that fantastic person you are.

A few weeks ago, I found out one of my friends was going through a situation in his life that I have been through in the same way. He had to take custody of his grandson because of his daughters' addiction to a drug. He has had him since he was a baby. I found out he is the same age as my grandson. I could never figure it out why he started talking to me on Facebook until we started talking. Then quickly I realized we were put into each other's lives. He has a girlfriend and has been with her for about ten years is what I am getting from the conversation. We both had a lot in common because of our grandchildren. The only difference is he's involved in a relationship. He is engaged, and I am seeing someone in a different way. We talked about a lot of different things going on in each other's lives and found out that some of the same things had happened or were in the process of taking place. Weeks went by and we stayed in touch and talked about our grandchildren and how they're growing and how much we love them. His daughter was released the same day mine was only to find out she did not do what she told her dad she would do. She is only hurting that little boy.

A month or two ago I spoke with my friend from Facebook to find out his engaged girlfriend of ten years was caught cheating on him. I really do not know the whole story of the situation, but I know he has been blown away by this situation in his life. I feel his hurt, but he needs his time to heal from this. I hope the two of them can work it out. If they do not, I would like for him to take time for himself and his grandson before he brings someone else into his life. I will always be there for him as a friend if he needs one. Good luck, Shortie!!!

Well, David and I went the first week of April 2021 to Alabama again to see his aunts. We drove my car this time and stayed over in South Carolina for the night. This trip started out totally different than the one before. David was a different person to me than on the last trip. I did not know how to take things, so I sat back and enjoyed the person he was this time. I saw more of a caring person in him than the last trip. I still am not sure how he feels or if he really does. I know that this time in my life I can relax and allow things to surface to the top. I need to know where I stand in this man's life. I want to be the one whom he decides to spend the rest of his life within this generation. I know they say time plays a huge factor, but how long do you need to carry on with someone to even know for sure if he is that one. I am a person who will not push a person to decide in their life, but when a heart gets involved, it becomes a challenge. The male friends that are in my life tell me it is time for him to step up to the plate. I am the type of person I do not like to push anyone because I do not like to be pushed. So…

Anyway, while on my trip with David I received a call from my mom's neighbor to inform me that my sister had passed, and my mom had a heart attack. While it was not how I wanted to begin that morning, David knew something was wrong and grabbed me to find out. As I told him about it, he held me and I felt the caring side of him I had never seen. Well, we had to get up and get packed so I could return home to see what and how things were. David drove most of the way except for when he had me to drive to get my mind off things. He was a true hero; he drove me straight through. What a wonderful person to do that for me. We made it to his house around midnight that night, so I just stayed there until morning. I was glad because I did not need to be by myself that night.

Well, the next morning I got up and headed home first to unload the car and head to the hospital to find out what happened and to check on my mom. Once I got there, I confirmed that my sister, Joyce, had passed, and my mom had a broken-heart attack and stents had to be put in. I would say that this was caused by finding my sister. Well, the next few months were in and out of the hospital with my mom. The new medications and all the procedures were taking a toll on her. Mom is not a person to take a lot of medication. Well, it has been since April 9th, 2021, and my mom is still not where she needs to be in her life. We are waiting on her to have more tests done to make sure that she did not have a mini stroke. So, in the meantime it is a standby thing until all tests have been completed in June.

Since all this happened David has come by a few times to see how my mom was doing or to see if she's improving. Things have changed in our friendship. He knew I had been through a lot myself and I really thought he was a more caring person than he was. I guess the two of us look at things such as caring in a different way. I can remember when his aunts called me to tell me how sick he was, and they were concerned, so for three days I went home from work and cooked a meal to take to him because he was too sick to cook. I do not really know what he thinks about things anymore. I stay so confused with the misleading vibes. Yes, he was honest about not being in a relationship because of his past. However how long does a person allow the past to dictate to them their happiness. I am going to close this book for now and will write another one later when life brings different things my way.

Well….

I am going to close this book for now to see what 2021 will bring in my life. Only God knows what is best for me….

CPSIA information can be obtained
at www.ICGtesting.com
Printed in the USA
BVHW081511131021
618855BV00015B/966